Grammar Plus

【Two-Page Edition】

大学英語『グラマー・プラス』
【コンパクト版】

Andrew E. Bennett
Toru Komiya

NAN'UN-DO

Grammar Plus: Two-Page Edition

Image Credits

All photographs © Shutterstock.com except:

p. 20 (vending machine) © infiksjurnal/Shutterstock.com

p. 20 (traffic jam) ©phichak/Shutterstock.com

p. 22 (high jumper) © sportgraphic/Shutterstock.com

p. 34 (race car) © Maxim Petrichuk/Shutterstock.com

Download Audio

音声ファイル
無料 DL
のご案内

このテキストの音声を無料で視聴（ストリーミング）・ダウンロードできます。自習用音声としてご活用ください。
以下のサイトにアクセスしてテキスト番号で検索してください。

https://nanun-do.com　テキスト番号［**512222**］

※ 無線 LAN（WiFi）に接続してのご利用を推奨いたします。

※ 音声ダウンロードは Zip ファイルでの提供になります。
お使いの機器によっては別途ソフトウェア（アプリケーション）の導入が必要となります。

Read by
Anya Floris
Chris Koprowski

※ Grammar Plus: Two-Page Edition 音声ダウンロードページは以下の QR コードからもご利用になれます。

本書の目的と構成

英語学習者にとって、文法は強力なツールとなります。時制やさまざまな品詞、そのほかの文法項目を学習することで、他者の考えを理解しながら、自分の言いたいことを口に出したり書いたりすることができるようになります。その一方で、文法は、単に決まりごとや規則を集めたものではありません。それは言語空間をすみずみまで満たし、私たちが読み、書き、聞き、話すことすべての中に存在します。言うなれば、文法こそ言語の血液なのです。

そこで登場するのが本書『Grammar Plus: Two-Page Edition』です。本書は、英語の基本的な文法項目をコンパクトにまとめた30のユニットで構成されています。それぞれの文法項目を説明するために実用的な例文がそのイメージを表わす写真とともに掲載されているので、それがしっかりと記憶にとどまります。さらに、数種類の演習問題を通して、英語の基本的な運用能力を強化しながら、日常生活で文法がどのように使われるのか学びます。本書は、文法の学習が楽しく、実用的で、達成感を感じられるものになることを意図して作られています。

以下は、Grammar Plus: Two-Page Edition のそれぞれのユニットを構成する要素の説明です。

各ユニットでは、学習する文法項目は2～3つのカテゴリに分けられています。たとえば、右に示したユニット（Unit 6：進行形）では、カテゴリは「現在進行形」「過去進行形」「進行形の疑問文」となっています。

まず、それぞれのカテゴリには3つの例文があり、文法項目が実際に使われる場面に対応した写真が添えられています。その下には、文法項目の働きと用法の説明があります。

例文を読み上げている音声は、データをダウンロードして聞くことができます。そのトラック番号は、ヘッドフォンのアイコンの下に示されています。

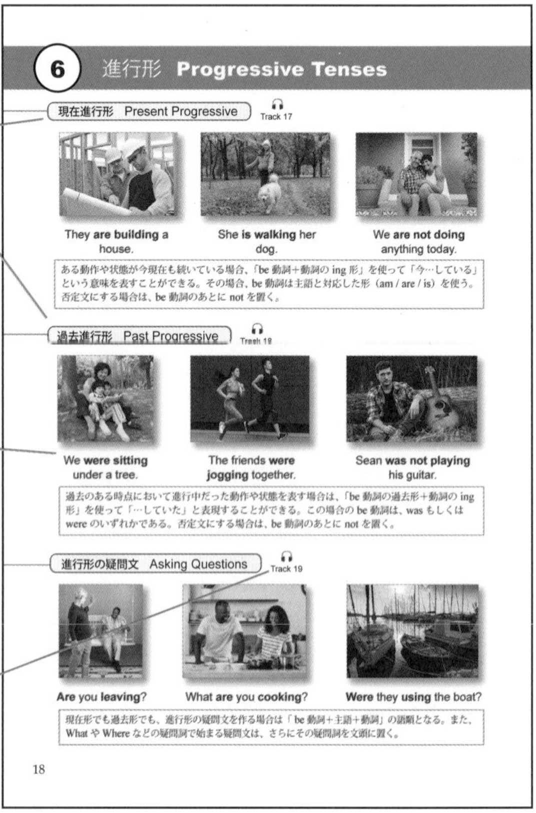
6 進行形 **Progressive Tenses**

現在進行形 Present Progressive Track 17

They **are building** a house. | She **is walking** her dog. | We **are not doing** anything today.

ある動作や状態が今現在も続いている場合、「be 動詞＋動詞の ing 形」を使って「今…している」という意味を表すことができる。その場合、be 動詞は主語と対応した形（am / are / is）を使う。否定文にする場合は、be 動詞のあとに not を置く。

過去進行形 Past Progressive Track 18

We **were sitting** under a tree. | The friends **were jogging** together. | Sean **was not playing** his guitar.

過去のある時点において進行中だった動作や状態を表す場合は、「be 動詞の過去形＋動詞の ing 形」を使って「…していた」と表現することができる。この場合の be 動詞は、was もしくは were のいずれかである。否定文にする場合は、be 動詞のあとに not を置く。

進行形の疑問文 Asking Questions Track 19

Are you **leaving**? | What **are** you **cooking**? | **Were** they **using** the boat?

現在形でも過去形でも、進行形の疑問文を作る場合は「be 動詞＋主語＋動詞」の語順となる。また、What や Where などの疑問詞で始まる疑問文は、さらにその疑問詞を文頭に置く。

18

Grammar Exercisesのセクションには、数種類の演習問題が掲載されています。ここでは、空欄補充問題、文の言い換え問題、誤り訂正問題、文の書き換え問題など、さまざまな種類の問題が用意されています。いずれの問題も、各ユニットの文法項目についての知識を確認し、その知識を使うことの自信を深め、論理的・客観的な思考力を養うことを目的としています。

Grammar Exercises

A (　) 内の指示に従って、次の文を書き換えなさい。

[例] I was resting.（現在進行形に）→ I am resting.

1. They cleaned their rooms.（過去進行形に）
   ____
2. We are watching TV.（否定文に）
   ____
3. Where do you live now?（現在進行形に）
   ____
4. He studies psychology.（現在進行形に）
   ____

B (　) 内に示された動詞と時制を使って、進行形の文を作りなさい。

[例] We _______ _______.（study・現在）→ We are studying.

1. She _______ _______.（sleep・現在）
2. All of my friends _______ _______.（dance・過去）
3. Bob and Kate _______ _______ _______.（play・過去＋否定）
4. One of us _______ _______.（go・現在）
5. What _______ you _______?（do・過去）

C 次の会話文の空欄に適当な語を入れなさい。

1. A: Hi, Rudolfo. Where (　　　　) you (　　　　)?
   B: Hey, Emily. I'm going to the supermarket.
2. A: Are you still helping Aaron?
   B: Yes, I (　　　　) (　　　　) him study for the test.
3. A: Kim looked sick yesterday morning. Was she feeling all right?
   B: No, she (　　　　) (　　　　) (　　　　) well. She went to the clinic in the afternoon.

19

『Grammar Plus: Two-Page Edition』をご利用の先生方へ:

本書をお選びいただき、誠にありがとうございます。先生方の授業の成功をお祈りするとともに、本書によって英語学習がさらに楽しく効果のあるものとなることを願っております。

本書で学習する学生の皆さんへ:

常に ベストを尽くしましょう。文法を学ぶ目的は、他者の考えを理解し自分が伝えたいことを表現するのに役立つ道具を手に入れるためであることを忘れないでください。皆さんは未来の世界のリーダーです。皆さんが自分の意見を自由に英語で発信できるようになることを期待しています。

楽しい英語学習を!

アンドルー E.ベネット

本書の姉妹書について

本書で扱っている文法項目を、読む、書く、聞く、話す、という4技能の観点から、より総合的に学ぶことができる『Grammar Plus第2版』という姉妹書があります。各技能の力を伸ばすための充実した各種演習問題に加え、英語の文法をさらに深く理解するための参照情報も提供しています。本書を学習したあとの発展学習用としても利用できます。

CONTENTS

1 be 動詞 “Be” Verb

様子や状態を表す（be ＋ (副詞＋) 形容詞） Describing Appearances and States

Track 2

She **is** surprised.

He **is** happy.

The road **is** closed.

be 動詞の現在形には am、are、is があり、主語が I のときは am を、you と they そして名詞の複数には are を、he、she、it そして単数の名詞には is を使う。否定文は be 動詞のあとに not を置いて作り、疑問文は主語と be 動詞の順番を逆にして作る。「主語 ＋ be 動詞 ＋（副詞＋）形容詞」という文では、その主語となっている人や物の様子や状態を表すことができる。

事実を述べる（be ＋名詞 (句) Giving Information

Track 3

They **are** good friends.

It **is** an elephant.

They **aren’t** doctors.

「主語 ＋ be 動詞 ＋ 名詞（句）」という文では、「主語 ＝ 述語」つまり「…（主語）は…（名詞）である」という情報を伝えることができる。

時間や場所などを示す（be ＋前置詞句／副詞） Indicating Locations, Times, etc.

Track 4

The ducks **are** in the pond.

The clock **is** on the wall.

The wedding **is** today.

be 動詞のあとに、日時や場所を表す語句を続けると、あることが起こる時間や、何かが存在する場所などを言い表すことができる。その語句には「前置詞＋名詞」または副詞が使われる。

Grammar Exercises

A 空欄にあてはまる be 動詞(現在形)を入れなさい。

[例] You ____________ a great dancer! → You are a great dancer!

1. She ____________ very friendly.
2. I ____________ 19 years old.
3. ____________ you the owner?
4. The keys ____________ not on the table.
5. ____________ it a good company?
6. We ____________ ready to go.
7. My sisters ____________ not here.

B (　)内の正しい語を選び、文を完成させなさい。

1. They (is / are) excited about the trip.
2. Tina and I (am / are) classmates.
3. The orange juice (is / are) in the refrigerator.
4. (Am / Are) I on time?
5. That (is / are) not Paul's bike.

C 次の文を読み、AとBのうち正しいほうを選びなさい。

1. Ted is a fast runner. Chuck is slow.
   (A) They are both fast.
   (B) Only one boy is fast.
2. The meeting time is 3:00 PM. We are ready to start. Ken is not here yet.
   (A) It is not time for the meeting.
   (B) Ken is late for the meeting.
3. Mr. Tanaka is at his office from Monday to Friday. His house is in Kobe. His office is in Osaka.
   (A) The house and the office are not in the same city.
   (B) Mr. Tanaka is in Osaka on Saturdays.

2 現在形 Simple Present Tense

反復する動作や日常の習慣を表す　Repeated Actions and Habits

Track 5

He **exercises** daily.

We **aren’t** open on holidays.

Do you **swim** here every morning?

毎日の通勤や通学などの反復する動作や日常の習慣などを言い表す場合には、動詞や助動詞の現在形が使われる。その場合、every day、anymore、always、sometimes、rarely、never などの頻度を表す副詞とともに使われることが多い。一般動詞の否定文は、do not (don’t) または does not (doesn’t) を動詞の前に置き、疑問文は do または does を文頭に置いて作る。

一般的な真理や事実を述べる　Truths

Track 6

There **are** five kittens in the box.

Sorry, I **don’t work** here.

Can I **pay** with a credit card?

不変の自然現象や科学的な真理、日常生活の中の客観的な事実を言い表す場合に現在形が使われる。

感情、知覚、所有を表わす　Feelings, Perceptions, and Possession

Track 7

The young girl really **likes** the story.

She **doesn’t know** the answer.

Do you **have** a copy of the report?

1. feel や like、hate などの動詞で人が現在経験している感覚や感情を表現する場合、2. believe、cost、know などの動詞で現在の状態を表す場合、3. have や own などの動詞で現在なにかを「持っている」という場合に現在形が使われる。

Grammar Exercises

A 次の文のあとに続く表現の記号を空欄に書き入れなさい。

1. Every day, I _______
2. The coffee machine _______
3. These cookies _______
4. Do you often _______

(A) makes four cups.
(B) watch movies here?
(C) taste delicious!
(D) wake up at 7:45.

B 次の会話文の空欄に適当な語を入れなさい。

1. A: __________ you always take the bus to work?
   B: On Mondays, I ride my bike. On other days, I __________ the bus.
2. A: I love this hat. __________ it come in other sizes?
   B: No, there __________ just one size. You can adjust it in the back.
3 A: How do you __________?
   B: I feel much better, thank you.

C (　　) 内に示された指示に従って、次の文を書き換えなさい。

[例] She plays the piano every day. (疑問文に)
→ Does she play the piano every day?

1. Are there a lot of people in the club? (肯定文に)

____

2. Gus hates waking up early. (否定文に)

____

3. The gym is open 24 hours. (疑問文に)

____

4. Aster doesn't work at the airport. (肯定文に)

____

5. They have coin lockers. (否定文に)

____

3 過去形 Simple Past Tense

過去形の肯定文と否定文 Positive and Negative Statements

Track 8

He **ate** a big breakfast.

There **were** some pretty balloons.

I **did not close** the door.

動詞の過去形は、過去のある時点における動作や状態、過去の習慣などを表すために使われる。be 動詞の過去形は was と were の２種類だが、一般動詞は動詞の原形に -ed を付けるもの（規則動詞）と、独自の形を持ったもの（不規則動詞）とがある。否定文を作るときは、be 動詞では was not (wasn't) か were not (weren't) を使い、一般動詞では、「did not (didn't) ＋動詞の原形」となる。

過去形の疑問文 Asking Questions

Track 9

Where **did** my car **go**?

Did you **enjoy** your meal?

What **did** Marco **say**?

過去形の疑問文は、be 動詞の場合は was か were を文頭に置いて作り、一般動詞の場合は did を文頭に置いて「Did ＋主語＋動詞の原形」のようにして作る。疑問詞を使った疑問文では、「疑問詞＋ did ＋主語＋動詞の原形」という形になる。

過去の習慣・継続的な状態 Used to

Track 10

This **used to be** a movie theater.

I **used to work** at that pizza restaurant.

She **didn't use to wear** hats. Now she always does.

過去の長い期間にわたる習慣について「昔はよく…していた」と言ったり、過去において長期間続いていた状態について「以前は…だったものだ」と説明したりする場合に、「used to ＋動詞の原形」が使われる。否定文は「didn't use to ＋動詞の原形」。

Grammar Exercises

A (　)内の動詞を過去形に変えなさい。

[例] We ____________ to him yesterday. (talk)

→ We talked to him yesterday.

1. She ____________ a bracelet and a pendant. (buy)
2. I ____________ not at my office this morning. (be)
3. You ____________ a beautiful garden. (plant)
4. The friends ____________ a bus to Yokohama. (take)
5. Mark and Francis ____________ not at the wedding. (be)
6. I ____________ to high school there. (go)

B 次の質問に対応する正しい返事を選びなさい。

1.	____ Did they pick up the package?	(A) No, they weren't.
2.	____ What did she say?	(B) We went to the beach.
3.	____ Were the shirts the right size?	(C) She said she may be late.
4.	____ Where did you go?	(D) Yes, they did.

C 次の文を読み、AとBのうち内容が正しいほうを選びなさい。

1. John lived in Kamakura from 2007 to 2010. In 2010, he moved to Hiroshima. He still lives there.
   (A) John used to live in Kamakura.
   (B) John lived in Kamakura in 2011.

2. Toru and Tina went to Phone World. Everything was too expensive. They decided to look for a phone online.
   (A) They bought a phone at Phone World.
   (B) They didn't buy anything at Phone World.

3. After university, Hideki got a job at a law firm. Eri joined the firm two years later. One year after that, Hideki changed jobs.
   (A) Hideki and Eri were classmates.
   (B) Hideki and Eri were co-workers.

4 代名詞 Pronouns

主語として使う代名詞 Subject Pronouns

Track 11

I work at a bank.

She doesn't live around here.

Did **he** walk home?

人や物を表す代名詞は、動作の主体、すなわち主語として使うことができる。語順は基本的に「主語＋動詞（＋目的語・補語）」となる。疑問文の場合は、do、does、did などの助動詞を先頭に置いて「助動詞＋代名詞＋動詞（＋目的語・補語）」とする。

目的語として使う代名詞 Object Pronouns

Track 12

Joe gave **her** flowers.

I didn't meet **him** in Italy.

Did Mom buy **it** online?

代名詞を動詞や前置詞の目的語として使う場合は、その直後に置かれる。ただし、人を表す人称代名詞の場合には、you 以外は次のように語形が変化する：I – me / we – us / he – him / she – her / they – them

所有を表す代名詞 Possessives

Track 13

The dog is **ours**.

That isn't **our** car.

Is this coat **yours**?

代名詞を使って「の…」という所有関係を表す場合は、「代名詞の所有格＋もの」という形をとる。また、it 以外の代名詞には、mine（私のもの）、yours（あなたのもの）というように、それだけで名詞の働きをする独立所有格がある。

Grammar Exercises

A 次の文には、代名詞が誤って使われている箇所があります。その代名詞に線を引き、正しいものを空欄に書きなさい。

[例] I am Chika. Here is me name card.

→ I am Chika. Here is ~~me~~ name card. ___my___

1. My name is Jack. My am from England. ________
2. There are so many bicycles here. Oh, that one is my. ________
3. Hi, Taro. It's so nice to see your! ________
4. I can't reach the salt. Can you please hand it to I? ________
5. These pants are great. Do them come in grey? ________
6. Where is him house? Isn't it in this area? ________
7. My dad bought I some nice gloves. ________

B (　)内の正しい語を選び、文を完成させなさい。

1. (He / Him) is my good friend.
2. Please give (she / her) my best wishes.
3. It's getting late. Stan and (I / me) need to wake up early tomorrow.
4. Do you want to see (my / mine) new purse?
5. I saw Theo today. I heard the news from (he / him).
6. These are really nice paintings. Were (they / them) done by a local artist?
7. Is this pen mine or (your / yours)?

C 空欄にあてはまる代名詞を入れなさい。

1. A: Is this your watch?
   B: No, it isn't. Maybe it's Anthony's. You should show it to ________.
2. A: I need to talk to Linda.
   B: I saw her a few minutes ago. ________ is in the library.
3. A: My phone is broken. Can I borrow ________?
   B: Of course. Here you are.

5 前置詞 Prepositions

時を表す前置詞 Time

Track 14

The concert starts **at** 7:30.

It doesn't snow **in** July.

Was it busy **on** Christmas?

英語には、時を表すための前置詞がいくつかあり、その使い分けを覚えておく必要がある。一般的な規則として、「…時に」では at、「…日に／…曜日に」では on、「…月に／…年に／春（夏・秋・冬）に」では in が使われる。after と since はどちらも「…のあとで」という意味だが、since は現時点まで「…からずっと」という継続の意味が含まれている。また、by と until も「…まで」という意味だが、by には期限、until には「…までずっと」という継続の意味が含まれている。

場所を表す前置詞 Location

Track 15

The boat is **under** the bridge.

The bag is **on** the floor.

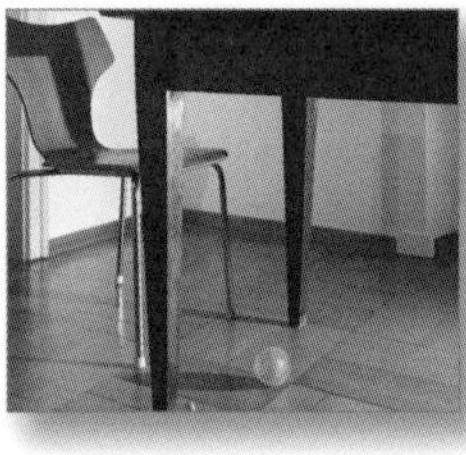

The chair is **beside** the table.

場所を表す前置詞でよく使われるのが at、in、on で、at は具体的な建物や「…番地」など、広がりのない狭い場所、in は市町村や区、県、地域、国などの範囲を表わす場所、on は「…に接触している」というイメージから、「…の上に」のほかに「…（川や湖）に面して」や「…（通り）沿いに」と表現する場合などに使われる。これ以外の前置詞についても、使い分けを整理して覚えておきたい。

その他の前置詞 Other Uses

Track 16

My co-worker is **against** the idea.

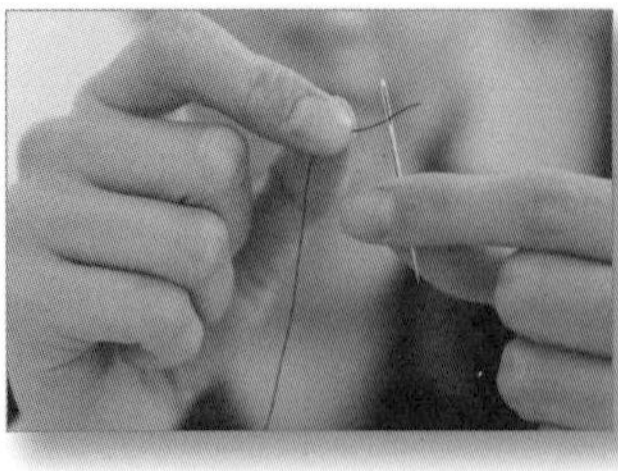

Put the thread **through** the needle, like this.

Did you walk **over** the little bridge?

前置詞は、時間や場所以外にもさまざまな意味を表すことができる。たとえば for は「…のために」、without は「…なしで」、against は「…に反対で」ということである。

Grammar Exercises

A 正しい前置詞を選んで、文を完成させなさい。

1. I will go to Sapporo (at / in) May.
2. They can park (in / on) front of the house.
3. The ball went (over / across) the fence.
4. We can't leave yet. We have to stay (by / until) 6:00.
5. Do you see the sign (by / up) the door? It says "No pets."
6. I love talking (between / with) Nate. He's a very interesting person.
7. I need some coffee. Otherwise, I might fall asleep (around / during) the movie.

B 次の文のあとに続く表現の記号を空欄に書き入れなさい。

1. I have karate class _____
2. The present is _____
3. Is there a bookstore _____
4. We are open from Monday _____
5. Can I ask you _____

(A) near the train station?
(B) to Saturday.
(C) at 4:30 PM.
(D) about this file?
(E) for my sister.

C 次の文を読み、AとBのうち正しいほうを選びなさい。

1. She has class from 2:00 to 3:45.
   (A) The class is over at 2:00.
   (B) The class lasts until 3:45.
2. My bank is on 4th Street. Further down the street, there is a grocery store. Even further down the street, there is a high school.
   (A) The school is next to the bank.
   (B) The store is on 4th Street. It is in between a bank and a school.
3. Chris wants to move to Okayama. Dana agrees with him.
   (A) Dana is for the idea.
   (B) Dana is against the idea.

6 進行形 Progressive Tenses

現在進行形 Present Progressive

Track 17

They **are building** a house.

She **is walking** her dog.

We **are not doing** anything today.

ある動作や状態が今現在も続いている場合、「be 動詞＋動詞の ing 形」を使って「今…している」という意味を表すことができる。その場合、be 動詞は主語と対応した形（am / are / is）を使う。否定文にする場合は、be 動詞のあとに not を置く。

過去進行形 Past Progressive

Track 18

We **were sitting** under a tree.

The friends **were jogging** together.

Sean **was not playing** his guitar.

過去のある時点において進行中だった動作や状態を表す場合は、「be 動詞の過去形＋動詞の ing 形」を使って「…していた」と表現することができる。この場合の be 動詞は、was もしくは were のいずれかである。否定文にする場合は、be 動詞のあとに not を置く。

進行形の疑問文 Asking Questions

Track 19

Are you **leaving**?

What **are** you **cooking**?

Were they **using** the boat?

現在形でも過去形でも、進行形の疑問文を作る場合は「 be 動詞＋主語＋動詞」の語順となる。また、What や Where などの疑問詞で始まる疑問文は、さらにその疑問詞を文頭に置く。

Grammar Exercises

A (　) 内の指示に従って、次の文を書き換えなさい。

[例] I was resting. （現在進行形に） → I am resting.

1. They cleaned their rooms. （過去進行形に）

____

2. We are watching TV. （否定文に）

____

3. Where do you live now? （現在進行形に）

____

4. He studies psychology. （現在進行形に）

____

B (　) 内に示された動詞と時制を使って、進行形の文を作りなさい。

[例] We ________ ________. （study・現在） → We are studying.

1. She ________ ________. （sleep・現在）

2. All of my friends ________ ________. （dance・過去）

3. Bob and Kate ________ ________ ________. （play・過去＋否定）

4. One of us ________ ________. （go・現在）

5. What ________ you ________? （do・過去）

C 次の会話文の空欄に適当な語を入れなさい。

1. A: Hi, Rudolfo. Where (　　　　　) you (　　　　　)?
   B: Hey, Emily. I'm going to the supermarket.

2. A: Are you still helping Aaron?
   B: Yes, I (　　　　　) (　　　　　) him study for the test.

3. A: Kim looked sick yesterday morning. Was she feeling all right?
   B: No, she (　　　　　) (　　　　　) (　　　　　) well. She went to the clinic in the afternoon.

7 名詞と冠詞　Nouns and Articles

数えられる名詞　Countable Nouns

Track 20

The **trees** are tall.

My **cat** doesn't like getting wet.

Do you have any **coins**?

「建物」や「場所」、「品物」など、具体的な形や範囲がある名詞は、数えられる名詞（可算名詞）として扱われ、それが複数ある場合にはふつう語尾に s が付けられる。英語の辞書では countable の頭文字「C」で示される。

数えられない名詞　Uncountable Nouns

Track 21

Would you like some **water**?

He doesn't take **sugar** with his coffee.

How can we get around this **traffic**?

「情報」や「時間」、「液体」など、まとまった形やはっきりした範囲を持たない名詞は、数えられない名詞（不可算名詞）で、複数形にすることはできない。辞書では uncountable の頭文字「U」で表される。

冠詞　Articles

Track 22

The Eiffel Tower is famous.

Would you like to see **a** photo of Luke?

Here is **the** contract you wanted to review.

不定冠詞の a や an は、1つのまとまった形のある名詞の前に付けられる。ただし、同じ名詞に再び言及するときは、定冠詞の the を付けて「その…」と表現する。状況から特定できるものには最初から the を付ける。また、特定の川、山、海、海峡、群島、砂漠などの地名や船、建物などの固有名詞の一部、「月」や「太陽」など自然界に1つしかない天体名の前には the が付けられる。

Grammar Exercises

A (　)内の正しい語を選び、文を完成させなさい。

1. It was (a / an / the) great game. Even better, our team won!
2. Please turn down (a / an / the) music. It's too loud.
3. A few (house / houses) in the neighborhood are 100 years old.
4. We have (space / spaces) in the back. You can put your things there.
5. Do you have (a / an / the) extra jacket? It's kind of cold outside.
6. This is the living room. Let me show you (a / an / the) kitchen.
7. I don't have any (money / moneys). I spent it all.
8. We played four (game / games) of Go. He won three of them.

B (　)内の名詞を必要に応じて正しい形に変えて空欄に入れなさい。

[例] a lot of ____________ (egg) → a lot of eggs

1. some ____________ (luck)
2. many ____________ (singer)
3. a few ____________ (child)
4. very little ____________ (ice)
5. three ____________ (bus)

C (　)内に a, an または the を入れなさい。

1. A: Oakdale is (　　　) small town. It's about 75 kilometers from here. We drove around (　　　) town yesterday. There are pretty oak trees along (　　　) main road.
   B: It sounds like (　　　) beautiful place.

2. A: How does (　　　) weather look today?
   B: I just checked my phone. There's good and bad news. There may be (　　　) rainstorm in the morning. But (　　　) weather should clear up by (　　　) afternoon.

8 助動詞 Modals

能力の度合いを示す　Levels of Ability

Track 23

She **can** jump very high.

He **can't** read it without his glasses.

Can you really fly a helicopter?

助動詞は動詞とともに用いられて、能力や可能性、必要性など、さまざまな意味をその動詞に付け加えることができる。その場合、助動詞とともに用いられる動詞は必ず原形となる。助動詞 can は「…することができる」という意味で、否定形は cannot (can't)、過去形は could、過去の否定形は could not (couldn't) となる。

可能性の度合いを示す　Levels of Probability

Track 24

All the bags **will** fit in the trunk.

I **might not** go on the river rafting trip.

Would 3:00 this afternoon be convenient for you?

助動詞の may (might) は、「…かもしれない」という何かが起こる可能性を示し、will (would) は、「…だろう」と、ある程度の確信をもって未来のことを予想する場合に使われる。 must は「…に違いない」という強い可能性を示す。なお、might、would は必ずしも過去のことを意味するわけではない。

義務の度合いを示す　Levels of Necessity

Track 25

She **ought to** clean her desk.

People **shouldn't** ride on the grass.

Do we **have to** finish today?

「…しなければならない、…すべきだ」という義務を表す場合に使われる助動詞がいくつかある。must は自分の意思でそう思っているときに、have (has) to はそれが規則だったり、仕方がないからしなければならなかったりするときに使われる。 ought to と should は、「義務ではないが…したほうがいい」という気持ちを表す。逆に、「…してもよい」という許可は may (might) で表わす。

Grammar Exercises

A 最初の文と逆の意味になるように、2番目の文の空欄に適切な語句を入れなさい。

[例] I will have a lot of free time. → I won't have a lot of free time.

1. I can translate the letter. → I __________ translate the letter.
2. Students shouldn't use a dictionary during the test. → Students __________ use a dictionary during the test.
3. We don't have to pay for the tickets to the game. → We __________ __________ pay for the tickets to the game.
4. Bikes must be left outside. → Bikes __________ __________ be left outside.
5. Guests have to return their trays after eating. → Guests __________ __________ __________ __________ return their trays after eating.

B (　　)内の正しい語を選び、文を完成させなさい。

1. The math problem is easy. I (can / can't) solve it.
2. We made the mess. We (must / ought / will) to clean it up.
3. The boy (shouldn't / couldn't) push the door open. It was too heavy.
4. (May / Would) I leave work early today? I need to go to the dentist.

C 次の文を読み、AとBのうちどちらの行動がとられる可能性が高いか選びなさい。

1. Some friends are going hiking tomorrow. Jack loves hiking. Tomorrow is his day off from work.
   (A) Jack can go hiking tomorrow.
   (B) Jack must not go with his friends tomorrow.
2. The restaurant is quiet at 6:30 PM. It gets very busy at 7:30 PM. It's hard to get a table then. Doris and her friends plan to eat there tonight.
   (A) To get a table, they must arrive at 7:30 PM.
   (B) To get a table, they should arrive at 6:30 PM.
3. Mike is going to a club on 5th Street. Parking is not allowed on that street. Parking is allowed on nearby streets.
   (A) Mike should park in front of the club.
   (B) Mike ought to park on 6th Street.

9 提案と命令 Suggestions and Commands

Let's を使った提案の表現　Suggestions Starting with "Let's"

Track 26

Let's get some hot chocolate!

Let's order cherry pie for dessert.

Let's give our teacher a basket of apples.

「Let's ＋動詞」で、その場にいる人に対して「いっしょに…しよう（じゃないか）」と提案したり、勧誘したりすることができる。否定文で「…しないようにしよう」という場合は、「Let's not ＋ 動詞」という語順になる。

提案を表す動詞　Subject + "recommend / suggest / think"

Track 27

The doctor **suggested** that I eat more vegetables.

I **think** we should cancel the picnic.

Mom **recommended** that I eat before the movie.

recommend や suggest などの動詞は、提案や勧誘の意味で使うことができる。その場合、提案の内容を表す that 節内の動詞（上の例文では eat と cancel）は原型のまま用いるか、その前に should を付けることになる。なお、think を使う場合は常に should を付ける。

命令文　Commands

Track 28

Please sign your name here.

Come take a look at this document.

Don't tap on the glass, or you'll bother the lion.

たいていの動詞はそのままの形で文頭に置くことにより、相手に対して「…しなさい」という命令や要求を表すことができる。ただし、please（どうぞ）を文頭か文末に追加することで、強い口調を和らげることができる。また「…してはいけない」という否定の命令文を作るには、「 Don't ＋ 動詞」という表現を使う。

Grammar Exercises

A （　）内に示された指示に従って、次の文を書き換えなさい。

[例] You should park somewhere else. （命令文に）→ Please park somewhere else.

1. Take the train. （提案を示す文に）

   I recommend that ______________________________

2. I think we should look for a new roommate. （let's を使った提案に）

   Let's ______________________________

3. I think you should drive more carefully. （命令文に）

   Please ______________________________

4. I recommend that you speak more slowly. （命令文に）

   ______________________________ , please.

B 次の文のあとに続く表現の記号を、空欄に書き入れなさい。

1. We're out of eggs. Let's _____
2. The library closes soon. Let's _____
3. He is an important client. Let's _____
4. It's about to rain. Let's _____
5. I need some cash. Let's _____

(A) hurry up and choose our books.
(B) do the best job possible for him.
(C) buy an umbrella.
(D) stop by the bank.
(E) go to the supermarket.

C 次の会話文の空欄に適当な語を入れなさい。

1. A: ________ throw a party next Friday.

   B: Good idea! Who should we invite?

2. A: Do you think I should get a new coffee maker?

   B: No, I ________ think you should. The one you have now is fine.

3. A: ________ turn down the television. I'm doing my homework.

   B: Sorry about that. I'll do it now.

10 未来形 **Simple Future Tense**

近い未来を表す現在形・現在進行形 Expressed with Present Tenses

Track 29

The store **closes** soon.

The ship **is leaving** shortly.

Are you **playing** golf again tomorrow?

未来のことでも、起こることが確実な場合には現在形が使われる。また、動詞の現在進行形を使うと、「…することになっている」というように、今、準備していることが近い将来に起こることを表すことができる。さらに、「主語 ＋ be going to ＋ 動詞の原形」を使うと、「…するつもりである、…するだろう」というように、近い未来の予定や予測を表すことができる。

will ＋動詞の原形 Will + Original Verb

Track 30

The race **will be** very close.

Someone **will fix** the air conditioner on Friday.

Will your parents **move** to this area?

それほど確実ではない未来について述べるときや、単に話者がそうなると思っているだけのときは、「主語＋ will ＋動詞の原形」で「…だろう」という表現を使うことになる。

未来形の否定文 Negatives

Track 31

The elevator **won't stop** on the second floor.

We **aren't going to see** the movie today.

The seller **will not reduce** the price.

未来形の否定文（…する予定はない、…しないだろう）は、be 動詞または will のうしろに not を付けて作る。いずれも isn't, aren't, won't のように短縮形が使われることが多い。

Grammar Exercises

A 未来のことについて述べている次の文の空欄に will、am、is または are を補いなさい。ただし、何も必要がないときは空欄のままにしておくこと。

[例] We ________ going to visit her next weekend.

→ We are going to visit her next weekend.

1. He ________ give us a ride to the airport.
2. No, I ________ not doing anything later.
3. ________ you be home this afternoon?
4. The plane ________ departs in 45 minutes.
5. She ________ moving to Miyazaki in August.

B 次の会話文の空欄に適当な語を入れなさい。

1. A: What ________ ________ doing over the holiday?

   B: I'm going ________ spend some time with my niece.

2. A: I see your sale starts on the 18th. ________ these pants be on sale, too?

   B: No, we just got those. They will ________ be on sale.

3. A: ________ Mary going with you to Berlin?

   B: It's mostly a business trip. So I ________ probably go alone.

C (　)内の指示に従って、次の文を書き換えなさい。

[例] He will be home tomorrow.（否定文に）→ He will not be home tomorrow.

1. You will have a lot of free time. （疑問文に）

   ____

2. I play racquetball with Ricky. （will を使った未来形に）

   ____

3. John is giving a presentation next Thursday. （否定文に）

   ____

4. She is leading a tour group to Australia. （疑問文に）

   ____

11 疑問詞と付加疑問文 Question Words and Tag Questions

疑問詞を使った疑問文　Question Words

Track 32

Where is the court house?

Who ate half the chocolate cake?

When will the bus get here?

疑問詞を使った疑問文では、疑問詞が文の先頭に置かれる。疑問詞が主語となっている場合では動詞が続き、それ以外の場合は主語と助動詞が倒置された文が続く。

How を使った疑問文　Compound Phrases with “How”

Track 33

How many calories are in one serving?

How often does the museum change exhibits?

How much does this washing machine cost?

how のうしろに状態を表す形容詞や副詞を続けて、さまざまな疑問文を作ることができる。長さを尋ねるときの How long、数を尋ねるときの How many、頻度を尋ねるときの How often、値段を尋ねるときの How much などは、その例である。

付加疑問文　Tag Questions

Track 34

There is enough room in the back, **isn’t there**?

This plant needs a lot of sunshine, **doesn’t it**?

You aren’t thinking about moving, **are you**?

付加疑問文とは、「…ですよね」「…ではないですよね」のように、相手に軽く念を押したり、同意を求めたりするために文末に追加される疑問文のこと。否定文には肯定の疑問を付け、肯定文には否定の疑問を付ける。主文に be 動詞が使われていればその be 動詞を、一般動詞や助動詞が使われていれば、時制や人称に応じて do / does / did や will や can などを使う。また、付加疑問文の中では、主語に対応した代名詞が用いられるが there 構文では there をそのまま使う。

Grammar Exercises

A (　　)内の正しい語を選び、文を完成させなさい。

1. (Where / Who / What) do you go to school?
2. How (long / much / many) time do we have?
3. (When / What / Whom) are they going to the farmer's market?
4. (Who / Where / What) is that man over there?
5. How (much / often / many) do you visit your aunt?
6. (Why / What / Who) is the road closed?
7. How (many / long / often) people are waiting in line?
8. (What / When / Where) are you doing this afternoon?

B 次の文に、付加疑問文を加えなさい。

[例] It's a good class, (　　　　　) (　　　　　)? → It's a good class, <u>isn't</u> <u>it</u>?

1. Slovenia is a beautiful country, (　　　　　) (　　　　　)?
2. The 100 yen shop closes at 8:00, (　　　　　) (　　　　　)?
3. You were born in Tokyo, (　　　　　) (　　　　　)?
4. They won't be late, (　　　　　) (　　　　　)?
5. The school doesn't have a website, (　　　　　) (　　　　　)?
6. Ben will meet us for breakfast, (　　　　　) (　　　　　)?

C 次の会話文の空欄に適当な語を入れなさい。

1. A: ______________ did you open the window?
   B: Because it's hot in here.
2. A: How ______________ bags do you have?
   B: I have two suitcases to check in. Also, I can take a bag on the plane, ______________ I?
3. A: How ______________ foreign languages does Frances speak?
   B: Let's see.... I know she speaks Spanish. She also speaks Italian, ______________ she?

12 形容詞 Adjectives

名詞を修飾する形容詞　Preceding Nouns

Track 35

It's an **old** piece of jewelry.

That isn't a **fast** train.

Should I just bring my **small** suitcase?

形容詞には、名詞の前に置かれてその名詞を説明したり、持続的な性質や状態を表したりする働きがある。これを「形容詞の限定用法」と言う。

主語の状態を表す形容詞　Following Linking Verbs

Track 36

The speaker looks **confident**.

The TV doesn't appear **broken**.

Did you get **tired** from climbing the stairs?

形容詞が、be 動詞や主語の状態・感覚を表す動詞のあとに用いられた場合は、その主語の一時的な状態を表すことになる。これは「形容詞の叙述用法」と言う。

数や量を表す形容詞　Quantifiers

Track 37

The man is following **several** horses.

There aren't **a lot of** people there.

Can I have **some** water, please?

数量形容詞には、複数形の普通名詞の前に置かれて数の大小を表すものと、物質名詞または抽象名詞の前に置かれて量や程度の大小を表すものがある。

Grammar Exercises

A (　)内の正しい語を選び、文を完成させなさい。

1. This pudding (tastes / feels) great. Did you make it yourself?
2. I love this photo. You (sound / look) happy standing there on the Brooklyn Bridge.
3. It (smells / turns) strange in here. There might be a gas leak.
4. Just tell me the truth. I won't (sound / get) angry.
5. He (appears / keeps) confused. Show him how to use the device.
6. I love your plan. It (sounds / becomes) perfect to me!
7. Do you (get / feel) all right? Your face is completely white.

B 次の文のあとに続く表現の記号を、空欄に書き入れなさい。

1. That book is wonderful. It's _____
2. He loves sports. So I bought him _____
3. She's going swimming. That's why she has _____
4. My fingers are not very big. I'll take _____
5. We want to go to Bali. Can you recommend _____

(A) a new baseball glove.
(B) this small silver ring.
(C) a good travel agent?
(D) my favorite story.
(E) that big towel.

C 次の文を読み、その内容を正しく表しているものをAとBのどちらかから選びなさい。

1. George works from Monday to Saturday. He also works on holidays.
   (A) George has a lot of free time.
   (B) George has little free time.
2. There were 500 tickets for the event. Nearly 490 are already sold.
   (A) There are many tickets left.
   (B) There are few tickets left.
3. John made eight bottles of hot sauce. He gave them all to friends.
   (A) John doesn't have any more hot sauce.
   (B) John still has some hot sauce.

13 比較 Comparatives

～と同じくらい as ... as ...

Track 38

Jenny is **as** tall **as** Tina.

I don't play chess **as** well **as** my father.

Are their cakes **as** delicious **as** their cookies?

2つのものを比較する場合、「A ＋ be 動詞 ＋ as 形容詞 as ＋ B 」という構文で、「A は B と同じくらい～だ」という意味を表すことができる。また、一般動詞に「as ＋副詞＋ as」を加えれば、程度を比較することができる。

比較 Comparatives

Track 39

The dog is **bigger than** the cat.

It isn't **more expensive than** the other restaurant.

Was the flight **less crowded than** you expected?

2つのものを比較する場合、「A ＋ be 動詞 ＋ 形容詞の比較級 ＋ than B 」という構文で、「A は B よりも～だ」という意味を表すことができる。一般に形容詞の比較級は、-er を語尾に付けて作るものと、形容詞の前に more または less を付けて作るものの 2 種類がある。

最上級 Superlatives

Track 40

Martin is the **strongest** person on our team.

It isn't the **largest** house around, but we love it.

Can I please have the **least spicy** curry?

形容詞の最上級を名詞の前に置くと「最も～な」という意味になる。複数のものの中で「A が最も～だ」ということは、「A ＋ be 動詞 ＋ the ＋形容詞の最上級 ＋ 名詞 」という構文で表すことができる。形容詞の最上級は、一般に -est を語尾に付けて作るものと、形容詞の前に the most または the least を付けて作るものの 2 種類がある。

Grammar Exercises

A (　)内の形容詞を必要に応じて適当な形に変えて空欄に入れ、文を完成させなさい。

[例] This apartment is ＿＿＿＿＿＿ than mine. (large)

→ This apartment is larger than mine.

1. For Atsushi, math is ＿＿＿＿＿＿ than science. (hard)
2. Our city has three theaters. This one is huge. It's the ＿＿＿＿＿＿ one. (big)
3. Your old car was as ＿＿＿＿＿＿ as a boat! (wide)
4. Good health is more ＿＿＿＿＿＿ than money. (important)
5. My office is ＿＿＿＿＿＿ than this one. It's so bright in here. (dark)

B 次のリストは、「形容詞、比較級、最上級」の順に並べたものである。空欄を埋めて、このリストを完成させなさい。

[例] big, bigger, ＿＿＿＿＿＿＿ → big, bigger, biggest

1. easy, ＿＿＿＿＿＿＿, easiest
2. smart, smarter, ＿＿＿＿＿＿＿
3. popular, more popular, ＿＿＿＿＿＿＿
4. ＿＿＿＿＿＿＿, cuter, cutest
5. common, ＿＿＿＿＿＿＿, most common

C 次の文を読み、その内容を正しく表しているものをAとBのどちらかから選びなさい。

1. Ted's house has three rooms. Jeff's house has six rooms.
   (A) Jeff's house is smaller than Ted's.
   (B) Ted's house is smaller than Jeff's.
2. Pencils cost 100 yen. Pens cost 125 yen. Markers cost 140 yen.
   (A) Pencils are cheaper than pens.
   (B) Pens are as expensive as markers.
3. The Nile River is 6,695 km long. The Amazon River is 6,400 km long. The Volga River is 3,700 km long.
   (A) The Amazon River is longer than the Nile River.
   (B) The Volga River is the shortest of the three.

14 副詞　Adverbs

動詞を修飾する　Modifying Verbs

Track 41

The race leader is driving **quickly**.

He isn't singing **quietly**.

Is it still raining **heavily**?

副詞は動詞（句）の意味を修飾する働きがある。「どれくらい」や「どのように」など、程度や状態を表わす副詞は、その動詞（句）のうしろに置かれることが多い。ただし、動詞に目的語がある場合は、その目的語のうしろに置かれる。

形容詞を修飾する　Modifying Adjectives

Track 42

She is **almost** ready to leave.

The theater isn't **very** big.

Is it an **especially** rare piece?

副詞は形容詞の意味を強めたり程度を表したりするために、その形容詞の直前に置かれる。ただし、enough だけは例外で、形容詞のあとに置かれる。

頻度・時・場所を表す副詞　Expressing Frequency / Time / Place

Track 43

We **frequently** eat at this restaurant.

He doesn't **usually** take the train.

Did they collect the garbage **yesterday**?

often（しばしば）や always（いつも）などの頻度を表す副詞は主語のすぐあとに置かれることが多く、tomorrow（明日）や yesterday（昨日）などの時を表す副詞と here（ここ）や there（あそこ）などの場所を表す副詞は文末に置かれることが多い。なお、時を表す副詞と場所を表す副詞が 1 つの同じ文の中で使われているときは、場所が先に来ることが多い。

Grammar Exercises

A (　)内の正しい語を選び、文を完成させなさい。

1. I see the elevator. It's over (there / that).
2. He (always / never) takes milk with his coffee. He prefers it black.
3. The door isn't (almost / very) wide. The sofa might not fit through.
4. Her songs are all (good / well) written.
5. Let's go (somewhere / nowhere) else. This place is too crowded.
6. Is that piece of wood (enough long / long enough)?
7. They aren't ready to start (already / yet).
8. Mr. Takara checked the document (carefully / careful).

B (　)内の単語を副詞に変えて空欄に入れなさい。

[例] It's a __________ growing trend. (quick) → It's a quickly growing trend.

1. The child __________ opened the present. (excited)
2. Their selection of reggae music is __________ good. (fair)
3. Passengers on a train should speak __________. (quiet)
4. The joke was __________ funny. (extreme)
5. Do you shop here __________? (regular)

C 次の文を読み、その内容を正しく表しているものをAとBのどちらかから選びなさい。

1. From Monday to Friday, Leon has French class every evening. Plus, he sometimes has private classes on the weekend.
   (A) Leon frequently studies French.
   (B) Leon rarely studies French.
2. I went to every store in town. None of them had that kind of paper.
   (A) The paper is sold everywhere.
   (B) The paper isn't sold anywhere.
3. I packed all my winter clothes into one box. I had to sit on it to close it!
   (A) The box was partially filled.
   (B) The box was completely filled.

15 不定詞 Infinitives

動詞＋不定詞 Following Certain Verbs

Track 44

Bob remembered **to lock** the door.

Natalie wasn't asked **to clean** her desk.

Do I have **to replace** any major parts?

「to＋動詞の原形」という形の不定詞を「…すること」という意味で用いると、いくつかの動詞のうしろに置いて目的語として使うことができる。「…しないこと」と否定する場合は、not を不定詞の直前に置く。have は「to ＋動詞の原形」が付くと助動詞の働きをして「～しなければならない」という意味になる。

動詞＋目的語＋不定詞 Following Objects

Track 45

Manuel taught her **to play** the guitar.

I didn't ask him **to dress** formally. It was his choice.

Do they want us **to turn off** our phones?

動詞の中には、間接目的語と直接目的語という 2 つの目的語をとるものがある。そうした動詞の中には、to 不定詞を「…することを」という意味で使い、直接目的語にできるものがある。その場合、「主語 ＋ 動詞 ＋ 間接目的語（人）＋ 直接目的語（不定詞）」という形をとることが多い。

形容詞＋不定詞 Following Certain Adjectives

Track 46

She is afraid **to walk** down the dark street.

The young boy isn't eager **to rake up** the leaves.

Are you ready **to have** fun?

いくつかの形容詞では直後に不定詞を続けて、「…をして…だ」と理由を示したり、「…をすることは…だ」という補足説明を加えたりすることができる。

Grammar Exercises

A （　）内の指示に従って、次の文を書き換えなさい。

[例] Did he decide to go on the tour? （肯定文に）

→ He decided to go on the tour.

1. They asked her to participate. （疑問文に）

2. He is willing to share the reward. （否定文に）

3. Allen doesn't want to buy a motorcycle. （肯定文に）

4. Did he remind Hiroaki to bring a flashlight? （肯定文に）

B 次の文のあとに続く表現の記号を、空欄に書き入れなさい。

1. The bag is too heavy. She _____
2. It's cold. Can you ask him _____
3. It was an important game. The athletes _____
4. I know it's a big secret. I promise _____
5. Many deer live here. They're easy _____

(A) to close the window?
(B) not to tell anyone.
(C) to spot in the forest.
(D) were proud to win it.
(E) doesn't plan to buy it.

C 次の文を読み、その内容を正しく表しているものをAとBのどちらかから選びなさい。

1. Today, Mark has a big test. He didn't study much. He doubts he will get many questions right.
   (A) He expects to pass the test.
   (B) He is prepared to fail the test.
2. Jenny received a text message. It was an invitation to Evan's party.
   (A) Jenny invited Evan to attend the party.
   (B) Evan invited Jenny to attend the party.
3. Their favorite band is coming to Tokyo. They slept outside to get tickets.
   (A) They are excited to see the band.
   (B) They were too scared to wait in line overnight.

16 動名詞 Gerunds

主語になる Subjects

Track 47

Hiking is a good way to get fresh air.

Biking in the rain isn't very fun.

Is **painting** houses a good way to make a living?

動名詞は動詞の原形に -ing が付いたもので、名詞としての働きを持つ。「…すること」という意味になって主語として使うことができる。

動詞の目的語になる Following Certain Verbs

Track 48

Today, the board discussed **expanding** into Mexico.

He hasn't finished **building** the fence.

How did you enjoy **traveling** to Kenya?

動名詞はいくつかの動詞の目的語として使い、「…することを」という意味を表すことができる。

前置詞の目的語になる As Objects of Prepositions

Track 49

The boy is learning about **gardening**.

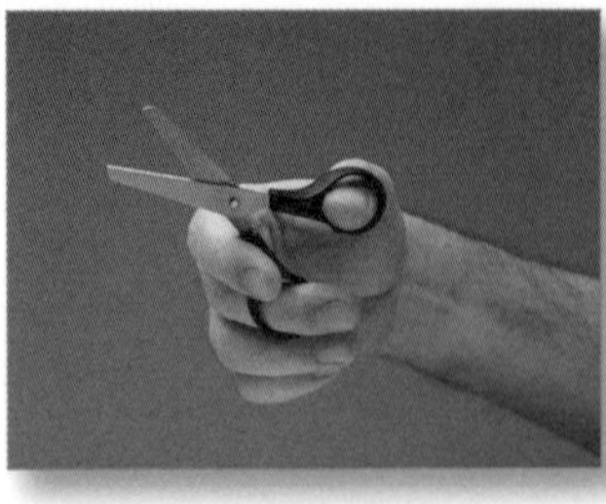

These scissors aren't the best for **cutting** cloth.

Is the speaker good at **explaining** his points?

by -ing（…することによって）、at -ing（…することにおいて）、in -ing（…することについて）などのように、動名詞は前置詞の目的語として使うことができる。

Grammar Exercises

A 次の各文には、誤りが 1 つずつ含まれている。その誤りに線を引き、正しい形を空欄に書きなさい。

[例] Grandparents always enjoy see their grandchildren.

→ Grandparents always enjoy ~~see~~ their grandchildren. ____seeing____

1. Visit museums is a great way to learn about history. ____________
2. The software is helpful for organize photos. ____________
3. We discussed spend the holiday in Seoul. ____________
4. How do you feel about train the new staff? ____________
5. Being an adult means take responsibility for your actions. ____________
6. Play the guitar helps me relax. ____________

B (　)内の正しい語句を選び、文を完成させなさい。

1. (Work / Working) in the entertainment industry is a lot of fun.
2. I'm sorry. I don't want (bothering / to bother / bother) you.
3. Thank you for (show / showing / to show) me the research center.
4. Do you remember (see / to see / seeing) the memo yesterday?
5. He can (meet / meeting / to meet) us at 4:30.
6. Our biggest challenge is (get / getting) enough signatures by Friday.

C 次の文が正しい文となるように、空欄に(　)内の単語を原形のまま、または不定詞か動名詞に変えて入れなさい。

1. A: What do you usually ____________ on the weekend? (do)
   B: Not much. I sometimes go bike ____________ with my sister. (ride)
2. A: Did Hiroshi decide ____________ at the animal shelter? (volunteer)
   B: He did. He really loves it.
3. A: This gadget is great for ____________ pancake batter. (stir)
   B: You're right! It would also ____________ perfect for cookie and cake mixes. (be)

17 接続詞 Conjunctions

複数の単語や語句を並べる　Compound Lists

Track 50

She makes delicious cookies **and** pastries.

We can cross here **or** use the underpass.

The hotel's restaurant is costly **but** delicious.

いくつかの単語や語句を対等な関係で並べるときには、A and B（A と B）や、A or B（A か B）を使う。並べる要素が３つ以上ある場合は、それぞれをカンマで区切り、最後のものの前にだけ and や or を置く（A, B, C, and D）。

複数の文を並べる　Compound Sentences

Track 51

Tomiko is studying business, **and** Paul is studying geology.

She wanted to shop at the store, **yet** it was closed.

There was supposed to be a game, **but** it started raining.

and は、複数の文を「そして…」と対等に並べたり、「それで…」と因果関係を示したりする場合に使われる。or は、別の選択肢を示す場合、but や yet は、前の文と相反することを述べる場合に使われる。

一対で接続詞となる語句　Phrases

Track 52

The bears are **not only** cute **but also** well made.

Either today **or** tomorrow is fine for me to meet up.

I'd **rather** have a snack **than** a full meal.

both A and B（A も B も）、either A or B（A か B のどちらか）、neither A nor B（A でも B でもない）、not only A but also B（A だけでなく B も）などのように、いくつかの語句が一対で使われて接続詞の働きをするものがある。なお、both A and B が主語のとき、動詞は A と B を合わせた数に対応し、それ以外の場合は、動詞は B の数に対応する。 なお、Not only A but also B の構文で A と B に文が使われる場合、A の文の主語と述語が倒置されることに注意。

Grammar Exercises

A (　　)内の正しい語を選び、文を完成させなさい。

1. For these sweaters, you can choose either red, black, (and / or / yet) white.
2. I'd be happy to help you move, (but / for / nor) I'm working all weekend.
3. (Either / Neither / Both) the pepper and the cinnamon are on the top shelf.
4. Sydney (for / and / nor) Paris both sound like amazing places to visit.
5. The heater is not only small (and / but / nor) also very warm.
6. We're new here, (or / also / and) we want to meet some neighbors.
7. Would you like milk (for / and / both) sugar with your coffee?
8. (Not / Neither / No) the salad nor the vegetable soup is fattening.

B 次の文のあとに続く表現の記号を、空欄に書き入れなさい。

1. I'd like to buy some pens, paper, _____
2. We can either watch a movie at home _____
3. Doris wants to get a cat, _____
4. These new phones are not only fast _____
5. The candle shop won't accept returns, _____

(A) but also stylish.

(B) nor will they let you exchange items.

(C) and a box of staples.

(D) or go to a theater.

(E) but her brother prefers dogs.

C 次の文の空欄に適切な接続詞を入れなさい。

1. A: What's the advantage of taking the train into the city?

   B: There are two. You can sleep on the train, __________ you don't have to look for a parking place.

2. A: Do you know where you're going to move yet?

   B: We're not sure. __________ we'll stay in the city, or we'll move somewhere near the ocean.

3. A: I love your backpack.

   B: Thanks! __________ __________ is it light, but it's also waterproof.

18 受動態 Passive Voice

能動態から受動態への書き換え From Active to Passive

Track 53

The sink **was fixed** by my nice neighbor.

This area **is enjoyed** by a lot of people in March.

Refreshments **will be provided** by a caterer.

動作を受けているものを主語にして文を作る場合、受動態を使う。そのときの文は「動作を受けているもの＋ be 動詞＋動詞の過去分詞」となる。否定文は be 動詞のあとに not を置いて作る。

助動詞のある受動態 Using Modals

Track 54

Phones **must be turned off** before the movie starts.

The temperature **can be adjusted**.

Due to the heavy snowfall, the art festival **may not be held**.

受動態の文で助動詞を使う場合、その助動詞は be 動詞の前に置き、be 動詞は原形のまま用いる。否定文では、not を助動詞と be 動詞の間に置く。

受動態の疑問文 Asking Questions

Track 55

What **was stolen** by the thief?

Will this item **be sold** in the auction?

Can the bicycle **be repaired**?

受動態の疑問文は、be 動詞を文頭に置いて作るが、助動詞を使う場合は、その助動詞を文頭に置く。疑問詞を使うときは、さらにその疑問詞を文頭に置く。ただし疑問詞が主語の場合は「疑問詞＋（助動詞）＋ be 動詞＋動詞の過去分詞」の語順となる。

Grammar Exercises

A (　　)内の指示に従って、次の文を書き換えなさい。

[例] A lot of children love the toy. （受動態の文に）

→ The toy is loved by a lot of children.

1. The entertainment will be provided by a band. （能動態の文に）

____

2. The volume should be turned up. （否定文に）

____

3. Their electricity was restored. （疑問文に）

____

B 次の文を、例にならって受動態に変えなさい。

[例] Many people use that service. → That service _____ _____ by many people.

That service is used by many people.

1. Someone must clean up the park. → The park must _________ _________ up.
2. Did the guard set the alarm? → _________ the alarm _________ by the guard?
3. Nobody changed the code. → The code _________ _________ _________.

C 次の文を読み、その内容を正しく表しているものをAとBのどちらかから選びなさい。

1. Mr. Kimura arrived at work at 8:15. In the parking lot, he saw a car with a broken window. He wrote down the license plate and told a security guard.
   (A) The window was broken by Mr. Kimura.
   (B) The broken window was reported by Mr. Kimura.
2. Diego and Luna went to a travel agency. They asked about vacations to Canada. An agent gave them details about several choices.
   (A) The details were provided by the travel agent.
   (B) The vacation was booked by the couple online.
3. Kaoru is selling her bike. She listed it online at a price of 10,000 yen. Someone offered her 6,000 yen. Kaoru feels that price is too low.
   (A) The offer will be accepted by Kaoru.
   (B) The offer will be rejected by Kaoru.

19 語源 Word Parts

よく使われる接頭辞 Common Prefixes

Track 56

The house is **sur**rounded by trees.

They haven't finished **pre**paring the meeting room.

Should he **re**place the old bike tires?

英語には、単語の前に付けられて、元の意味を補ったり変えたりする接頭辞がいくつかある。たとえば、auto（自ら）が mobile（移動する）と組み合わされて automobile（自動車）という意味になる。よく使われる接頭辞の意味を知っていると、初めて見る単語でもその意味を推測できることがある。

よく使われる語根 Common Roots

Track 57

The price de**pend**s on the weight.

He doesn't usually play this **ver**sion of the game.

How many images does the **vis**ual dictionary have?

単語の基本的な意味を表す部分を「語根」といい、さまざまな接頭辞や接尾辞と組み合わされて、別の単語が作られる。たとえば、bio（生、生命）という語根を持つ単語に、biology（生物学）や biography（伝記）、antibiotic（抗生物質）などがある。

よく使われる接尾辞 Common Suffixes

Track 58

Next, I add sugar to sweet**en** the pudding.

The outfit may not be suit**able** for the party.

Is he a professional pian**ist**?

語の末尾に付けて、意味を加えたり、品詞を変化させたりする接尾辞がいくつかある。

Grammar Exercises

A (　)内の正しい語を選び、文を完成させなさい。

1. Arthur isn't afraid of anything. He is (fearing / fearless / fearful).
2. We are a leading (production / produce / producer) of light bulbs.
3. Nell is a (perfectionist / perfectly / perfect). Everything must be exactly right.
4. The pen is (refill / refillable / refilling). It's easy to add more ink.
5. With this new information, we'll need to (modify / modifier / modification) the report.
6. Our (supply / supplies / supplier) is great. He's never late with shipments.
7. I'm sorry for not being (cared / careful / careless). I left the sink running.

B 次の単語の意味を(A)〜(E)の中から選び、その記号を空欄に書きなさい。

1. _____	prediction	(A) plentiful / having a lot of something
2. _____	induce	(B) make longer
3. _____	bountiful	(C) another possibility or choice
4. _____	alternative	(D) a guess about something before it happens
5. _____	lengthen	(E) make happen / get someone to do something

C (　)内の単語を正しい形に変えて空欄に入れなさい。

1. A: What a great ___________! (perform)
   B: I agree. It was a fantastic show.
2. A: What's the ___________ between this city and the ocean? (distant)
   B: About 50 kilometers. Some ___________ have small boats. (reside) They take them out to the ocean every month or so.
3. A: I don't understand the ___________ of this TV show. (attract)
   B: I really like it. All the ___________ are excellent, and so is the director. (act)

20 形容詞節 Adjective Clauses

人物の説明を加える People

Track 59

The man **who designed this building** is famous.

The person **that bought the painting** is not from this area.

Is Liza the director **who won a bunch of awards**?

人を表す名詞や代名詞があるとき、そのうしろに who、that、whom、whose などの語句を続けて形容詞節を作り、その人についての説明文を加えることができる。

場所の説明を加える Places

Track 60

Is this the place **where you and Jack usually go**?

The farm **which will host the celebration** isn't near any highways.

Is this the restaurant **that serves free desserts**?

場所を示す名詞があるとき、うしろに where や which、that などの語句を置いて形容詞節を作り、その場所についての説明文を加えることができる。

動物・物の説明を加える Things and Animals

Track 61

This is the bus **that goes downtown**.

Iguanas aren't the type of pet **which many people want to raise**.

Is this the book **that you were looking for**?

動物や物を表す名詞の場合は、うしろに which または that を置いて、説明文を加えることができる。

Grammar Exercises

A (　)内の指示に従って、次の文を書き換えなさい。

[例] It is the town where the movie was filmed. (否定文に)

→ It is not the town where the movie was filmed.

1. He is the person who leads the group. (疑問文に)

____

2. Are these the shells which she found at the beach? (平叙文に)

____

3. The bus that goes to the convention center is comfortable. (否定文に)

____

4. It's not the shop whose owner just turned 90. (肯定文に)

____

B (　)内の正しい語を選び、文を完成させなさい。

1. Let me show you some dresses (which / who) we just got in.
2. The man (who / whom) lives across the street is a lawyer.
3. Do you know any places (where / which) I can get handmade soap?
4. This information is for travelers (that / whose) visa is about to expire.
5. The person to (whom / where) the flowers were sent was not home.

C 次の文の空欄にwho、whom、which、whose、whereのいずれかを補いなさい。

1. A: Is Detroit the city ____________ you two met?
   B: Actually, no. We met in San Francisco. I attended a conference ____________ Mary organized.

2. A: The company is looking for someone ____________ speaks Arabic.
   B: I studied Arabic for three years. Maybe I should apply for the job.

3. A: Elizabeth Barrett Browning is someone ____________ writing I admire.
   B: I recently read something which you might already know. The person for ____________ she wrote many poems was her husband, Robert.

21 副詞節 Adverb Clauses

時を表す Time

Track 62

Danica will go out **after the weather improves**.

Once she felt better, Alice took a short swim.

While Maya stacked the fruit, Tim brought more out.

時間を表す接続詞のあとに主語と動詞を続けて、時を表す副詞節を作ることができる。上の最初の例文のように、未来のことでも副詞節の中の動詞は現在形になることに注意。

原因・理由を表す Causal Relationships

Track 63

Because there is only one bank machine, there is a line to use it.

The store will gift wrap the shirt **since it is a present**.

As he had nothing else to do, he washed his car.

あるできごとの原因や理由を表すため、as や because、since などの接続詞を使って「…だから」「…のため」という意味の副詞節を作ることができる。

ことがらを対比する Contrast

Track 64

She will buy the ring **even though it is expensive**.

Although the lake was a little crowded, we rented a boat.

Mike is a big soccer fan, **whereas his best friend Annie loves basketball**.

although や even though、whereas など、ことがらを対比させる接続詞を使って、「…だけれども」「…にもかかわらず」という意味の副詞節を作ることができる。

Grammar Exercises

A （　）内の正しい語(句)を選び、文を完成させなさい。

1. (Once / Although) the economy is bad, they want to invest in real estate.
2. The hillside is beautiful (after / even though) the flowers bloom.
3. (Now that / Whereas) he has his own studio, the photographer can start looking for clients.
4. It isn't safe to look at your phone (before / while) you drive.
5. They need to find a new dentist (since / when) their current one is retiring.
6. (Though / After) the roadwork is completed, traffic will be smoother.

B 次の文のあとに続く表現の記号を、空欄に書き入れなさい。

1. Once it was warm enough, _____
2. As we're buying a house, _____
3. They leave the heater on all night _____
4. I will book the plane ticket _____
5. Because there were no seats, _____

(A) we applied for a loan.
(B) after the trip dates are set.
(C) he had to stand the whole way.
(D) Sara went out for a walk.
(E) even though energy costs are high.

C 次の文を読み、AとBのうち内容が正しいほうを選びなさい。

1. Nobuyuki talked on the phone for 15 minutes. Then he put on his coat. Finally, he walked to the bus station to meet his friend.
   (A) Before Nobuyuki met his friend, he talked on the phone.
   (B) Nobuyuki talked on the phone as he walked to the bus station.
2. At the stadium, Ivan asked about opening day tickets. They were all sold out. He decided to look for tickets on the Internet.
   (A) Ivan bought tickets at the stadium since they were available there.
   (B) As the stadium was out of tickets, Ivan tried to get some online.
3. We warned Junko about buying stock in the hi-tech company. She bought some stock anyway. A month later, the company went out of business.
   (A) After people warned her, Junko stayed away from the stock.
   (B) Junko bought the stock even though people advised her not to.

22 仮定法 Conditionals

可能性の高いことを仮定する Real / Possible Situations

Track 65

If my stylist **is** available, I **will get** a haircut tomorrow.

He **might take** an express train **if there is** one leaving soon.

If she **finishes** work by 5:30, she **will go** jogging.

「もし…ならば…する」というように、ある条件とその結果を単純に述べる場合は、「If ＋主語＋動詞の現在形、主語＋（助動詞）＋動詞の原形」という構文が使われる。

事実に反すること、可能性の低いことを仮定する Unreal / Impossible Situations

Track 66

They **would take** a ferry across the lake **if** the service **were offered**.

If we **had** more space, we **could fit** more desks in here.

If their star player **had not been** hurt, the team **might have won** more games.

現在の事実に反することを仮定して、「もし…ならば…するのに」と言うときは、if 節の中の時制を過去にし、結論部分は「主語＋ would（could, might, should）＋動詞の原形」を使って表現する。このとき、if 節の中に be 動詞が使われていたら、主語が I や it、he、her であっても were が使われることが多い。また、過去の事実に反することを仮定して、「もし…だったら…したのに」と言うときは、if 節の中の時制を過去完了にし、結論部分は「主語＋ would（could, might, should）＋ have ＋動詞の過去完了形」を使う。

Grammar Exercises

A (　)内の正しい語(句)を選び、文を完成させなさい。

1. They will visit their cousin if there (was / is) time.
2. If I (were / was) you, I would listen to Mr. Lin's advice.
3. If we decide to remodel the room, we (will / would) hire an interior decorator.
4. If they (have / had) provided food, the reception would have been better.
5. We may move the tournament to a larger location if more people (sign / signed) up.
6. I would (transfer / have transfer) to another department if I had a choice.
7. If the server (goes / went) down, our IT expert can fix it.

B 次の文のあとに続く表現の記号を、空欄に書き入れなさい。

1. If the spa offers the service, _____
2. He would go scuba diving _____
3. We would have invited you _____
4. They may offer drama classes _____
5. If I didn't need my car today, _____

(A) I would let you use it.
(B) if enough students want to take them.
(C) if he didn't have to work.
(D) if we had known you liked river rafting.
(E) she will get a massage.

C 次の文を読み、AとBのうち内容が正しいほうを選びなさい。

1. If Gregory had the power, he would change the policy.
   (A) Gregory doesn't want to change the policy.
   (B) Gregory doesn't have the power to change the policy.
2. They will plant some orange trees if there is room on the property.
   (A) They may plant some orange trees.
   (B) There is definitely not enough room for orange trees.
3. If the trail had not been closed, they would have hiked to the waterfall.
   (A) It was possible to hike to the waterfall, but they didn't do it.
   (B) They were not able to visit the waterfall.

23 名詞節 Noun Clauses

目的語となる As Objects

Track 67

He is trying to figure out **who made the sculpture**.

I don't know **how they fit so many toys on the shelves**.

I finally learned **where that mysterious tunnel goes**.

主語と動詞を備えた 1 つの文が、「…ということ」という意味のひとかたまりの名詞の働きをするものを名詞節という。名詞節は目的語として使うことができる。名詞節を作るときは、関係代名詞 what、疑問詞、that や whether などの接続詞が使われ、節の中の語順は「主語＋述語」となる。

主語となる As Subjects

Track 68

How we're going to arrive on time is an excellent question.

That the stadium improved their food selection is welcome news.

When the water level will recede is hard to say.

名詞節は、主語として使うこともできる。その場合、名詞節は常に単数として扱われる。

疑問文の中で使う Asking Questions

Track 69

Do you know **what this jacket is made of**?

Can you tell me **where the light bulbs are**?

Are you sure **there are no more flights to Geneva today**?

疑問詞で始まる名詞節は、疑問文の中で使って具体的な質問の内容を表すことができる。

Grammar Exercises

A (　)内の正しい語を選び、文を完成させなさい。

1. I'm not sure (where / why) the mall is. I'll look for the address online.
2. (How / What) we are supposed to raise one million yen in two weeks is a very good question.
3. Did she say (when / where) she's coming back? The coffee shop closes soon.
4. We're still trying to determine (what / why) the power went out.

B (　)内の指示に従って、次の文を書き換えなさい。

[例] He knows what the formula is. （疑問文に）

→ Does he know what the formula is?

1. It worries me that summers are becoming so hot. （名詞節を文頭に置いて）

    ____

2. We believe what Dan told us. （否定文に）

    ____

3. Do the police know who committed the crime? （平叙文に）

    ____

4. Why the road is still closed isn't clear. （名詞節をうしろに置いて）

    ____

C 次の文の空欄に、適切な単語を入れて名詞節を作りなさい。

1. A: Can you tell me ________ the shift manager is?

   B: Sure. It's Mr. Nakamura. Do you need to talk to him?

2. A: That was an interesting meeting. Judith didn't say ________ we might open a new branch. Is it going to be in Singapore?

   B: Probably, but I'm not sure ________ the plan will go forward. It might not be until July.

3. A: ________ they made changes to the schedule so late bothers me.

   B: I know ________ you mean. The planning could be a lot better.

24 現在完了 Present Perfect

過去の経験や完了した行為・出来事を表す　Past Actions

Track 70

I **have received** the samples.

The studio **hasn't finished** filming the movie.

Have you **given** the dog a bath this week?

「…し終わった」「…したことがある」と、現在から見て過去の行為や出来事について述べるときは、現在完了形を使う。現在完了は、have (has) のあとに動詞の過去分詞を置いて作る。否定文は have (has) のあとに not を加えて作り、疑問文は文頭に Have (Has) を置いて作る。

過去から現在までの継続を表す　Duration

Track 71

She **has been** there more than 20 minutes.

The panda exhibit **hasn't been** open long.

How long **have** you **worked** as a bee keeper?

「これまで…していた」と、過去のある時点から現在まで継続している行為や状態を表す場合にも、現在完了が使われる。その場合、since ...（…以来）や for ...（…の間）などの期間を示す語句が添えられることが多い。「これまでどれくらい？」と、期間を尋ねる場合は、疑問詞を使って How long have (has) ... ? のように尋ねる。

現在完了の文でよく使われる副詞　Common Adverb Pairings

Track 72

The school has **rarely** seen such a gifted athlete.

I'm afraid I haven't spoken to Hikari **recently**.

Have you **ever** played against that team?

already（すでに）、never（一度も）、ever（これまでに）、just（たった今）、recently（最近）、often（しばしば）、rarely/seldom（めったに…ない）、since（…以来）、certainly（間違いなく）など、現在完了とともによく使われて、その意味を補足する副詞がいくつかある。

Grammar Exercises

A 次の文を、(　)内の動詞を使って現在完了の文にしなさい。

[例] She ________ ________ here since 9:30. (be)

→ She has been here since 9:30.

1. I ________ not ________ the new baby videos yet. (upload)
2. Two of my friends ________ already ________ the exhibition. (see)
3. How long ________ you ________ as an executive assistant? (work)
4. John and Donovan ________ ________ in Japan since 2003. (live)
5. ________ he ever ________ a solo art show? (have)

B (　)内の正しい語(句)を選び、文を完成させなさい。

1. Most of the candidates (has / have) submitted their proposals.
2. Karen has (become / became) very good at her job.
3. We have (ever / never) gone scuba diving.
4. How many plays (you have / have you) acted in?
5. The deadline (already has / has already) passed.

C 次の文を読み、AとBのうち内容が正しいほうを選びなさい。

1. From 2016 to 2019, Hoshina was a student at the London School of Economics. As a student, he worked very hard. He wanted to visit Cambridge and York in England, but he didn't have the time. Now he is back in Japan.
   (A) Hoshina has never visited York.
   (B) Hoshina has been to Cambridge.
2. From 2001 to 2009, Laurie lived in New York. In 2009, she moved to Boston. She still lives in Boston.
   (A) Laurie has lived in New York since 2001.
   (B) Laurie has lived in Boston since 2009.
3. They started painting the office at 8:00 AM. At noon, they took a break for lunch. Then they continued their task. They are still painting the office.
   (A) They haven't finished painting the office.
   (B) They haven't had lunch yet.

25 過去完了　Past Perfect

過去の出来事の発生順　Sequencing Past Actions

Track 73

We arrived at 8:30. The party **had** already **started**.

Shortly into the camping trip, we realized we **hadn't brought** enough food.

Is the scratch something you **had seen** before renting the car?

過去完了は、過去のある時点を基準として、それ以前に起きた出来事を表わす。完了形を作る助動詞 have を had にし、その後に動詞の過去分詞を続けると「(過去のある時点までに)…し終えていた／ずっと…だった」という意味になる。

名詞句の中の過去完了　With Noun Clauses

Track 74

We suspected the equipment **had been tampered with**.

After returning from vacation, Jeff noticed the office **had been rearranged**.

Were you aware the host **had expanded** the guest list?

主節の動詞が過去形で目的語に名詞節をとる場合、その名詞節内で示されている出来事が主節の動詞以前に起きたことをはっきり示したいときに過去完了形が使われる。

過去完了進行形　Past Perfect Progressive

Track 75

By the time the food came, we **had been waiting** 45 minutes.

I **hadn't been living** in the area long, so the earthquake was surprising.

Was the supply shortage a problem you **had been anticipating**?

「…したときまでずっと…していた」のように、過去のある時点まで、何らかの動作がその前から続いていたことを表わす場合に過去完了進行形が使われる。その文は「had ＋ been ＋現在分詞」の形をとる。

Grammar Exercises

A (　　)内の動詞を過去完了の形にして、文を完成させなさい。

[例] We arrived at the theater at 8:15. The play _______ already _______. (start)

→ We arrived at the theater at 8:15. The play had already started.

1. Originally, I ___________ ___________ to take a train to Prague. (plan) I changed my mind and took a plane instead.

2. There weren't enough chairs because the event organizers ___________ only ___________ 50 people to attend. (expect)

3. Did you say you ___________ ___________ to finish by 5:00? (hope)

4. Before yesterday's video chat, they ___________ not ___________ for 12 years. (speak)

B 次の文のあとに続く表現の記号を、空欄に書き入れなさい。

1. Before the nail salon closed, I had _____
2. Greece was perfect. We had been _____
3. Gwen had heard the garden _____
4. Do you know why they had been _____

(A) looking forward to traveling there for a long time.
(B) considering changing the date?
(C) been working there for 11 years.
(D) was full of roses and lilies.

C 次の文を読み、AとBのうち内容が正しいほうを選びなさい。

1. In the middle of the outdoor festival, it started to rain. We got wet since we had expected the weather to be nice all day.
   (A) Before the festival, they knew it was going to rain.
   (B) They probably didn't bring umbrellas or raincoats to the festival.

2. Michelle had never dreamed of becoming a world-famous pop star. Her success surprised her as much as anyone else.
   (A) Michelle had not planned to become so well known.
   (B) Since she was a child, Michelle's goal was to become famous.

3. Anthony, the restaurant's owner, had been doing all the food deliveries himself. Eventually, he hired a driver to handle deliveries.
   (A) Anthony was hired by the restaurant to deliver food.
   (B) After hiring a driver, Anthony didn't need to deliver food himself.

26 未来完了 Future Perfect

時を示す表現とともに使う Using Time Markers

Track 76

By dinner time, he **will have finished** painting the fence.

At 4:00 PM, the store **will not have closed** for the day.

Will they **have completed** the bridge's construction before July 15?

「(…までには) …していることだろう」のように、未来のある時点までに何らかの動作が始まっていたり、完了していたり、経験していたり、状態が継続したりしている場合に未来完了が使われる。その文は「will ＋ have ＋過去分詞」の形をとる。

現在形との併用 With the Present Tense

Track 77

The office **will have been cleaned** before the CEO arrives.

As soon as I collect one more signature, I **will have filled up** the whole sheet.

When Bob speaks with Lisa, **will** he **have met** with everyone in the department?

主節の文で未来完了が使われていても、時や条件を表す副詞節や形容詞節の中では、未来の出来事であっても will を使わずに現在形を用いる。例えば、上の文では、それぞれ will arrive や will collect、will speak などとしないこと。

未来完了進行形 Future Perfect Progressive

Track 78

At 3:45, he **will have been waiting** there exactly two hours.

By winter, this train line **will have been operating** for 25 years.

When the clock strikes 10:00, the guard **will have been standing** there three hours.

未来のある時点においても現在の出来事が引き続き進行中であることを表わす場合に、未来完了進行形が使われる。その文は「will have been ＋現在分詞」の形をとる。

Grammar Exercises

A (　　)内の動詞を未来完了形にして、それぞれの文を完成させなさい。

[例] By Friday, the schedule will ________ been ________. (determine)

→ By Friday, the schedule will have been determined.

1. As soon as someone buys this muffin, I will ________ ________ out of my baked goods. (sell)
2. Experts fear the company will not ________ ________ its distribution problems by the start of the third quarter. (solve)
3. Will they ________ ________ the roadwork by the time the monsoon season begins? (complete)

B (　　)内の指示に従って各文を書き換えなさい。

[例] She will have left by 3:30.（否定文に変更）

→ She will not have left by 3:30.

1. The limited-edition shoes will not have sold out.（肯定文に変更）

____

2. Will the rule have been changed before the tournament starts?（平叙文に変更）

____

3. They will have announced the ceremony's date by Sunday.（疑問文に変更）

____

C 次の文を読み、その内容を正しく表しているものをAとBのどちらかから選びなさい。

1. Roy needs to get here soon. In 20 minutes, all of the food will have been eaten.
   (A) If Roy arrives in 30 minutes, he won't have anything to eat.
   (B) There is plenty of food left, so there's no need for Roy to rush.
2. By next year, they will have been working on the project for eight years.
   (A) They have been working on the project for more than five years.
   (B) It's going to take another eight years to finish the project.
3. The gala is on the 25th. By the 23rd, the palace will have been decorated.
   (A) It will not be possible to decorate the palace before the date of the gala.
   (B) The palace will be decorated before the gala takes place.

27 間接・直接話法 Indirect and Direct Speech

間接話法（過去時制の場合） Indirect Speech (with the past tense)

Track 79

Francine **said** she loved the striped sweater.

Everyone **said** they wanted to stay at the beach longer.

Lindsey **told** me she planned to move to a bigger place.

間接話法とは、人が発言した内容を、それを伝える者の立場から間接的に表現する方法。その内容は、say、tell、ask などの伝達動詞のあとで that（しばしば省略可）、if、whether などの節の中で示される。基本的に、伝達動詞が過去であれば、その後の節の中の動詞も過去となる（時制の一致）。

間接話法（異なる時制との組み合わせ） Indirect Speech (with other tenses)

Track 80

Manny **said** he eats a large, green salad every day.

The artist **told** the reporter he's working on a new series of paintings.

My classmates **answered** they would love to form a study group.

間接話法は、さまざまな時制と組み合わせて使われる。伝達動詞が過去でも、発言の内容が現在でも変わらない事実や習慣であれば現在形、継続中であれば現在進行形が使われる。

直接話法 Direct Speech

Track 81

Kip's mom **said**, "Watch your brother while you're at the park."

The lifeguard **shouted**, "Everybody get out of the water!"

The little boy **asked**, "What ice cream flavors do you have?"

直接話法とは、発言した人の言葉をそのまま引用する形で表したもので、その部分を引用符（“ ”）で囲む。引用部分は伝達動詞のうしろ、前、その両方のいずれの位置にも置くことができる。

Grammar Exercises

A (　)内の正しい語を選び、文を完成させなさい。

1. After the flight, Dad (said / told) he felt tired.
2. Lana (told / said) she will get the car dent repaired soon.
3. “Ms. Wilson,” the interviewer (reported / asked), “what’s the main reason you want to work here?”
4. I asked about the store’s holiday hours. The salesperson (told / said) me they are open on holidays until 6:00 PM.
5. I (asked / shouted) how much the cheese cost. The grocer said it depends on the type and weight of the cheese.

B 次の文のあとに続く表現の記号を、空欄に書き入れなさい。

1. The painter said he will _____	(A) the office will be closed all week.
2. When I called, a recording said _____	(B) try and pay attention.”
3. Ms. Endo said, “We’ll reply _____	(C) you deliver the sofa today?”
4. “Tim,” the teacher said, “please _____	(D) to your request by Friday.”
5. The customer asked, “Can _____	(E) finish the job tomorrow.

C (　)内の指示に従って、それぞれの文を書き換えなさい。

[例] Lydia said she will attend the wedding.（直接話法に）

→ <u>Lydia said, “I will attend the wedding.”</u>

1. Bill said, “I will meet everyone at the theater.”（間接話法に）

____

2. Kenji told us his goal is to become the CEO of a big company.（直接話法に）

____

3. My colleague asked me when the meeting will start.（直接話法に）

____

4. The man said, “The hotel is fully booked.”（間接話法に）

____

28 文と文をつなぐ語句 Transitions

因果関係を表わす Causation

Track 82

Business was booming at the bakery. **Therefore**, it hired several more people.

It has been a cold and dry winter. **Because of that**, my skin is dry.

There weren't enough chairs. **For that reason**, some people had to stand.

前の文を受けて、「その結果…」という原因と結果の関係を表わす副詞（句）がいくつかある。因果関係を表わす副詞には、therefore「それゆえに」、accordingly「したがって」、so「そういうわけで」、then「それで」などもある。

対比を表わす Contrast

Track 83

This hardware store has great deals. **In contrast**, other places are more expensive.

Not everyone is here yet. **Regardless**, we need to start the meeting.

The road is rough. **However**, our truck can handle it.

「A は…。その一方で B は…」のように 2 つの文を対比する副詞（句）がいくつかある。上の例以外に、by contrast「それとは対照的に」、on the contrary「一方」、meanwhile「その一方で」、unlike「…とは違って」などがある。

情報を追加する Addition

Track 84

Our cats love to be petted. **Likewise**, our dog asks everyone for attention.

I need two buckets of paint. **Additionally**, I'd like a paint roller, please.

The repair work will be difficult, **not to mention** time consuming.

すでに述べたことに情報を追加するときに使う表現がいくつかある。also、likewise、plus、(then) again、on top of this/that、besides、furthermore などもよく使われる。分詞構文を使って「とは言うものの、…」を意味する Having said that,... のような慣用句もある。

Grammar Exercises

A (　)内の正しい語(句)を選び、文を完成させなさい。

1. There was a hole in the roof. (Because / Because of that), water came in when it rained.
2. The price of the drill is a little over our budget. (Had / Having) said that, it would last a long time.
3. The parade will feature a marching band. (Additionally / Addition in), there will be giant balloons.
4. Bus fares went up. (As a result / Resulting), bus ridership decreased.
5. Those curtains are heavy and dark. (Contrasting / In contrast), these are light and bright.

B 次の文のあとに続く表現の記号を、空欄に書き入れなさい。

1. It was her first-ever soccer match. _____
2. We ran out of paper. Because of _____
3. Manuel will be promoted. _____
4. There was an accident, hence the _____
5. I was in favor of the merger. _____

(A) Moreover, he will receive a pay raise and a company car.
(B) Nevertheless, she scored a goal.
(C) However, Jack was against it.
(D) that, I couldn't print the document.
(E) big traffic jam on the highway.

C 次の文を読み、その内容を正しく表しているものをAとBのどちらかから選びなさい。

1. The power went out during the storm. Consequently, the house was completely dark last night.
   (A) The house's lights went out before the storm.
   (B) The storm caused the lights to go out.
2. I understand everyone is tired. Regardless, we need to finish today.
   (A) They must finish today even though everyone is tired.
   (B) Because everyone is tired, they will finish another day.
3. During the hike, the path will be steep, not to mention narrow.
   (A) Although the path will be steep, it will not be narrow.
   (B) The path will be both steep and narrow.

29 助動詞＋現在完了 Modal + Present Perfect

過去の可能性を表わす Possibility

Track 85

The customer **may have decided** to buy a computer elsewhere.

Someone **could have placed** the bucket here in case the roof leaks.

Might the ring **have been turned in** to the lost and found counter?

過去の可能性について、may [might] や could などの助動詞を使って自分の判断を加える場合、それが過去の出来事についてのものであれば、「助動詞＋ have ＋過去分詞」の形をとる。

過去の確実性を表わす Certainty

Track 86

I **must have dropped** the bag in the movie theater.

The little toy **can't have cost** 12,000 yen. It's made of plastic.

The suitcase **couldn't have come open** by itself. We wrapped two straps around it.

確実性を表わす助動詞には、その度合いの高いものから must「…に違いない」、should「きっと…だろう」、can [could]「…のはずだ」、may [might]「…かもしれない」などがある。過去の出来事について判断を下す場合は、「助動詞＋ have ＋過去分詞」の形をとる。その場合、can よりも could、may よりも might の方が確信の度合いが低くなる。

後悔や残念な気持ちを表わす Regrets and Lost Opportunities

Track 87

I **should have asked** for permission before borrowing the bike.

Danny **shouldn't have bought** stock in that energy company.

Could the town **have prevented** the recent landslide?

「…すべき［できたはず］だったがそうしなかった」という後悔の気持ちを表わすには、「should ＋ have ＋過去分詞」（…すべきだった）や「could have ＋過去分詞」（…できたはずなのに）を使う。

Grammar Exercises

A 「助動詞＋完了時制」を使って、それぞれの文を完成させなさい。(　　)内の動詞を使うこと。

[例] The lock's combination must __________ been __________. (change)

→ The lock's combination must have been changed.

1. The amusement park's website may not __________ been __________ with the new opening hours. (update)
2. I should __________ __________ the revised schedule on the wall. (post)
3. The new employee couldn't __________ __________ the printer. (break)
4. Might a nail __________ __________ the tire puncture? (cause)
5. We could __________ __________ to a larger house, but we didn't. (move)

B 次の文を読み、その内容を正しく表しているものをAとBのどちらかから選びなさい。

1. This bank should have installed a wheelchair ramp years ago.
   (A) Years ago, a ramp was installed by the bank.
   (B) The bank did not install a ramp years ago.
2. The detective may have found an important clue in his investigation.
   (A) It's possible that the detective found an important clue.
   (B) An important clue was definitely found.
3. The berries must have been eaten by a deer.
   (A) It's almost certain that a deer ate the berries.
   (B) It's hard to say what happened to the berries.

C (　　)内の指示に従って、次の文を書き換えなさい。

[例] The fundraiser may have reached its goal. (否定文に)

→ The fundraiser may not have reached its goal.

1. A construction worker could have dug this hole. (疑問文に)

   ____

2. I shouldn't have changed my phone number. (肯定文に)

   ____

3. Tina must have locked the safe. (否定文に)

   ____

30 紛らわしい語句 Similar Pairs

LikeとAs (Like and As)

Track 88

The little boy walks **like** a duck.

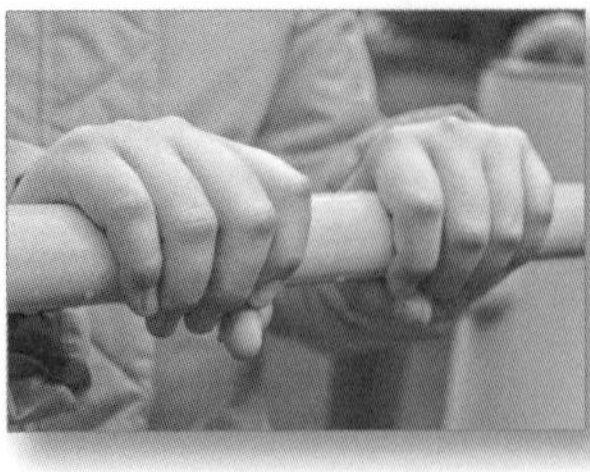

This metal bar feels **as** cold **as** a stone.

It looks **like** the bottle leaked during shipping.

as と like は似た意味を持つが、用法は大きく異なる。as は「as ＋形容詞（副詞）＋ as」の形で「…と同じくらいの」という意味を表わす。like は前置詞として名詞の前に置かれると、「…のような［に］」という意味になる。

DuringとWhile (During and While)

Track 89

I almost fell asleep **during** the speech.

While my dad cooked, I set the dinner table.

After a **while**, the car alarm stopped.

どちらも一定の期間を表わすために使われるが、during は前置詞なので名詞（句）が続く。while は接続詞で、しばしば進行形の文が続く（主語が主節のものと同じ場合は「主語＋ be 動詞」を省略できる)。また、while は名詞として「時間、期間」という意味もある。

SuchとSo (Such and So)

Track 90

You are **such** a good listener.

These blueberries taste **so** good!

It was **so** cold that I put on a jacket.

such は主に形容詞として名詞（句）の前で「そのような、たいへんな」、so は副詞として形容詞の前で「そんなに、とても」の意味を表わす。どちらも後に続く語句を強調するために使われる。「so ＋形容詞＋ that ...」の構文は「とても…なので…」という意味の頻出表現。

Grammar Exercises

A (　)内の正しい語を選び、文を完成させなさい。

1. Does that sound (like / as) a helicopter to you?
2. What are you going to do (while / during) summer vacation?
3. The juice is (so / such) sweet because it has pineapples in it.
4. Samantha's grandmother used to say to her, "You look as pretty (as / like) a picture."
5. (During / While) we're waiting for Cleo, tell me about your weekend.
6. After winning the match, the ping pong player was (such / so) excited that she jumped up and down.

B 次の文のあとに続く表現の記号を、空欄に書き入れなさい。

1. To move the big rock, he pushed as _____
2. Do you usually try to sleep _____
3. We were surprised that the beach _____
4. Is it all right if I put my clothes _____
5. The magic show was such a success _____

(A) during long flights?
(B) that the promoter added more dates.
(C) away while we talk?
(D) hard as he could.
(E) was so crowded today.

C 次の文を読み、その内容を正しく表しているものをAとBのどちらかから選びなさい。

1. As the weather was poor, Joe took a train instead of riding his bike.
   (A) Joe always rides his bike, even in bad weather.
   (B) Because of the weather, Joe decided not to ride his bike.
2. While waiting for meals, guests can listen to a live band and dance.
   (A) If guests want, they can dance before they eat.
   (B) The band does not play when the restaurant is open.
3. The low-budget movie was so good that it won several awards.
   (A) The movie had a chance to win awards but wasn't successful.
   (B) Even though the movie had a small budget, it was award-winning.

Grammar Plus: Two-Page Edition [B-966]
大学英語『グラマー・プラス』【コンパクト版】
1 刷 2024年 1月 22日

著 者	アンドルー E. ベネット	Andrew E. Bennett
	小宮 徹	Toru Komiya
発行者	南雲 一範 Kazunori Nagumo	
発行所	株式会社 南雲堂 〒162-0801 東京都新宿区山吹町361 NAN'UN-DO Co., Ltd. 361 Yamabuki-cho, Shinjuku-ku, Tokyo 162-0801, Japan 振替口座 : 00160-0-46863 TEL: 03-3268-2311(代表)/FAX: 03-3269-2486 編集者 加藤 敦	
製 版	Andrew E. Bennett	
装 丁	Nスタジオ	
検 印	省 略	
コード	ISBN978-4-523-17966-5 C0082	

Printed in Japan

E-mail nanundo@post.email.ne.jp
URL https://www.nanun-do.co.jp/

Grammar Plus
【Second Edition】
Andrew E. Bennett Toru Komiya
大学英語「グラマー・プラス」[改訂新版]
Nan'un-do

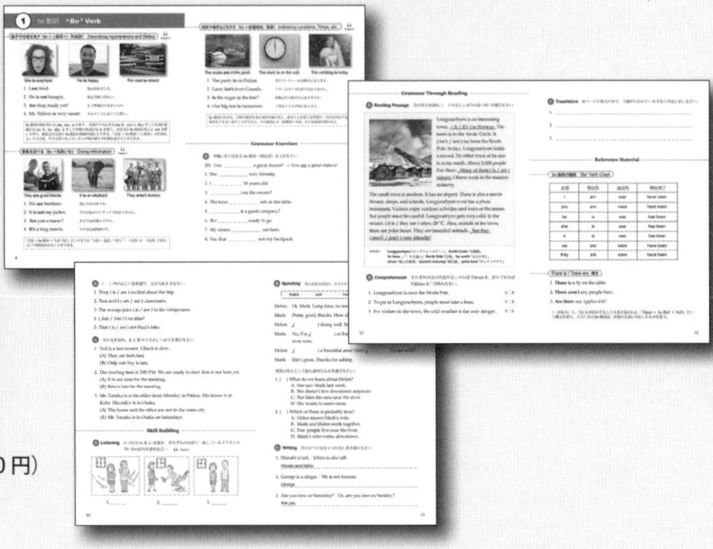

MP3 CD付
イラスト＋写真で1ヵ月スピードマスター
英文法『イメトレ』
Andrew E. Bennett／小宮徹 著
She is surprised.
The dog is extremely large.